My shapes

FUNdamentals series
BY MARIA YIANGOU

My shapes book.
Written and Illustrated by Maria Yiangou
Creative Director C.Y.
Cover by Maria Yiangou

info@idovedesign.com

Please subscribe at: www.idovedesign.com
to be notified of any free book offers,
discounts, book releases & promotions.

I have 3 sides.

triangle

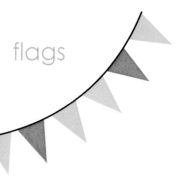

flags

clothes hanger

sandwich

I can be used to show direction.

arrow

ONE WAY

sign

arrow

I am round and have no corners.

circle

wheel

orange

clock

button

I look like the shape of the moon.

crescent

moon

banana

horse shoe

croissant

I have 1 line crossing the other.

cross

first aid

sign

I have
10 sides.

decagon

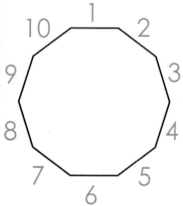

I look like a kite.

diamond

kite

diamond ring

sign

heart

I am the shape of love.

symbol of love

four leaf clover

strawberry

I have
7 sides.

heptagon

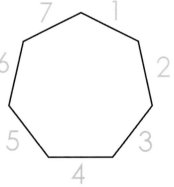

I have 6 sides.

hexagon

honeycomb

nut and bolt

I have no corners and shaped like an egg.

oval

egg

football

olive

watermelon

I have 5 sides.

pentagon

bird house

sign

rectangle

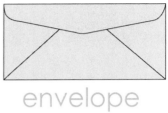

envelope

door

note pad

I have many pointy sides.

star

sheriff's badge

starfish

cookies

xmas tree star

nonagon

I have
9 sides.

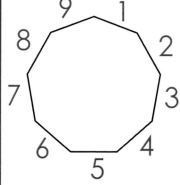

I have 8 sides.

octagon

sign

trampoline

semicircle

kettle

igloo

I have 4 equal sides.

square

frame

stamp

slice cheese

2 dimensional shapes

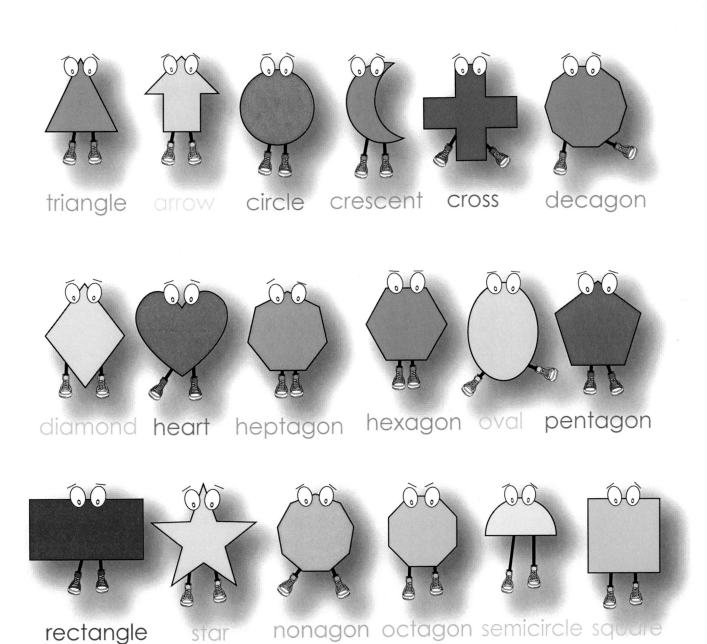

triangle   arrow   circle   crescent   cross   decagon

diamond   heart   heptagon   hexagon   oval   pentagon

rectangle   star   nonagon   octagon   semicircle   square

I look like an ice cream cone.

cone

ice cream cone

party hat

traffic cone

cube

I am the shape of a square box.

box

dice

ice cube

alphabet blocks

cuboid

I am the shape of a brick.

brick

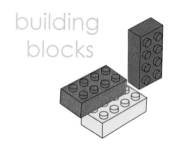
building blocks

book

fish tank

I look like a can of food.

cylinder

can of food

battery

drum

pot plant

pyramid

I look like a pointy tower with triangle sides.

pyramids

candle

tent

sphere

I am
round like
a ball.

ball

yarn

earth

3 dimensional shapes

cone

cube

cuboid

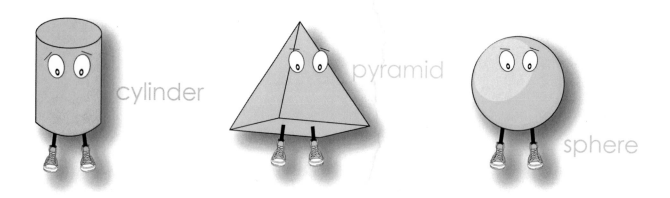

cylinder

pyramid

sphere

THE END

Please leave a review if you enjoyed this book.
Your feedback helps make our books better :)

Made in the USA
San Bernardino, CA
09 September 2018